© Sakura Book Publishing, Durban, South Africa.
www.sakurabookpublishing.com
alta@sakurabookpublishing.com

Poetry is Not Dead
ISBN: 978-1-0370-4644-5 (print)
978-1-0370-4645-2 (e-book)

**Poetry is not dead**

# FOREWORD
## Ekta Somera
# EDITING AND CURATING
## Alta H. Haffner
## Ekta Somera

# Authors

| | |
|---|---|
| Alta H. Haffner | Yaseen Adam |
| Charles R. Haffner | Tamia Moonsamy |
| Ekta Somera | Sthuthukile Mkhize |
| Maria Mortimer | Kinjal Vithal |
| Zain Omarjee | Zahida Wahab |
| Lezel Simons | Vishnu Kristna |
| Vinoo Nydoo | Richard J. Mann |
| Zoë-Lin Akkiah | Nikki Naicker |
| Vanessa Govender | Bianca Nikita |
| Anthee Ramlucken Sukai | Busisiwe Ngwenya |
| Padmini Govender | Neermala Devi Moodley |
| Sonia Naidoo | Vijayan Vengadachellam |
| Sevani Singaram | Nokanyiso Msani |
| Farah Messi | Saroj Moodley |
| Vee Dilrajh | Sinobom Vutha |
| Donna-Marie | Selwyn Anderson |
| Sanjana Singh | Brett Fish Anderson |

# FOREWORD
# BY EKTA SOMERA

It is rumoured that poetry is a dying art, and there are whispers on the street that poetry books do not sell. This book is a challenge to that notion.

Each poem in this collection encapsulates the beating heart of the poet, from tangling sentences and personifying the mundane, to bringing alive metaphors through descriptive imagery. The simple gesture of writing makes a bold statement as the title of this book conveys, poetry is not dead.

I have had the privilege of watching many of these poets grow and flourish in their own writing journey, and I am honoured that this collaboration could bring together our unique experiences through a shared collection of words.

In this digital era, with technology drawing our attention in different directions, it is easy to lose sight of the things that truly matter. Literature, poetry, and art remind us of what it really means to be alive. It brings us into the moment we are living in and helps us to find a sense of clarity in the middle of utter chaos.

As you read through these pages, I hope you are reminded for the first time or for the hundredth, that poetry is a living and breathing force, essential to capture the unseen beauty, that is necessary to understand and appreciate our very own existence in this world.

# ALTA H. HAFFNER

**Alta H. Haffner is a Haiku poet whose work captures the essence of precious, fleeting moments with simplicity and depth. Born with a deep appreciation for the beauty of brevity, Alta's Haiku poems reflect her keen observation of nature and her ability to evoke emotions in just a few short lines.**

**Drawing inspiration from the ever-changing seasons, the delicate balance of the natural world, and the quiet whispers of every new dawn, Alta's Haiku poems invite readers to slow down, pause, and appreciate the present moment. With a handful of syllables, she allows her readers to contemplate.**

**Her passion will always be to inspire other writers to get their books published to an international audience. "I believe all writers should have a book with their name on it" ~ Alta H Haffner**

**Tiktok: @poetaltahhaffner**

## SADNESS

I know darkness,
I feel grief so deeply,

Not just for my loss,
but yours ~
and theirs

Sadness is my winter that refuses to leave.

## WAITING ~ HAIKU

pretty butterfly
contemplating in the sun
waiting for the rain

# CHARLES R. HAFFNER

Charles R Haffner was born in Baltimore Maryland and lived in Central Florida for 15 years. For the past two years, he has written numerous books consisting of various forms of micro poetry.

His books can be found on amazon.com and he is the co-owner of Sakura Book Publishing with his wife Alta H Haffner. He resides in South Africa.

Thunderous clapping
Of gigantic ears, an old
Elephant keeps cool.

All night shining bright
Reflections of their star's love
In moon beams tonight.

Slow dance or floating petals
surrounding these gifts of Japan.
Pink patches healing the hurting
eyes silently staring each day.
Children standing under the trees as
they hold easter baskets.

# EKTA SOMERA

**Ekta Somera is a South African youth activist, author and founder of Paper Trail Literary Journal. She turns visions into reality on a daily basis, bringing books to life, while living her own dream at Sakura Book Publishing. Kindness and humility are the core values that guide her heart. Ekta's books are titled, Made in Poetry and Twenty-Two, each collection encapsulates her journey as she navigates through the complexities of life. Her latest collection, Social Misfit, both challenges and heals, encouraging readers to fiercely embrace who they are.**

**Outside the world of books, she's deeply involved in youth advocacy, especially around youth unemployment. Her insightful opinion pieces on social issues and youth concerns have been widely published, and she has been featured as a panelist on prominent media platforms. Ekta was named among the Mail & Guardian's 200 Young South Africans in 2022 and she was awarded the Youth Icon Award at the Lotus FM Women of Substance Awards in 2024.**

**Tiktok: @ektasomera**

# DEAD POETS SOCIETY
# BY EKTA SOMERA

The constellations are maddening
to the deranged lovers
begging the dying stars
to align one more time

There is a resonance to longing
for an experience
captured in the memory
of our scattered minds

To live in this world
we must bring alive
the dead poets
immortality to survive.

# MARIA MORTIMER

Maria Mortimer is 19 years old and was born and raised on a family farm in the Eastern Cape, South Africa. She has been heavily involved in the farm work for as long as she can remember and used to travel two hours to and from school every day. During these hours, Maria would dream up the next poem to write, often inspired by the people around her. She began writing poetry at the age of ten. Writing has not always been easy, as she is dyslexic. However, Maria is grateful to God for surrounding her with her incredible family and friends, who have supported her throughout her writing journey.

# POETRY IS NOT DEAD
# BY MARIA MORTIMER

Poetry is not dead
Not the words scrawled
Like tears not yet shed
As the pen crawls

No.

Poetry is not dead
Not the laughter
In the letters shared
As the ink writes "ever after"

No.

Poetry is not dead
Not the grief
That couplets fear to tread
And paper is an emotional thief

No.

Poetry cannot be dead
Can you not feel the heartbeat?
As the poem is read?
The sonnet has no seat
And did you see the alphabet bled
From every mark the poet said? -

Poetry is not dead...

# THE WORDS
# BY MARIA MORTIMER

The words keep coming
Like flashes from cameras
At a crime scene,
And they cannot stop...
Numerous strings of letters
Pumped out of hearts to form poetry
And flowing like ink-tinted blood
Onto the veins of the page.

Poetry is not dead,
For it sustains its poet,
Forms the heartbeat.
Creation is in its creator,
Such as a leech is to poetry,
To a mortal human,
That the poetry lives on...
And cannot die...

# ZAIN OMARJEE

Zain Omarjee is a poet, traditional artist and educator currently based in Johannesburg, South Africa. With a passion for pencil and pen traditional artwork, exploring identity, nature, and the combination of auditory storytelling and visual sketch work, his work has been featured in the literary journal entitled, "PaperTrailZA".

Zain earned an Honour's Degree in Bachelor of Arts in Motion Picture Medium, where he was honoured with the Best Producer award and the Critic's Choice award for Best Film. In addition to his writing, Zain is actively involved in mentoring emerging filmmakers. His work often reflects personal and artistic influences such as a love for the natural world, the fluidity of the pen, and how spirituality intertwines with every aspect of existence.

Zain's contributions to this anthology explores the intersection of healing through poetry and the resilience of the human spirit. He is currently working on a collaborative art project, and his writing continues to evolve as he seeks to challenge stereotypical conventions of the self from a South African perspective and connecting with other likeminded creatives. A Special thank you goes out to Ekta Somera for this opportunity to be a part of this fantastic series.

IG: zain.omarjee

# POETRY AS A HEALING BALM
# BY ZAIN OMARJEE

Underneath the pressure of skies both old and blue,
I sketch truths in verses, borrowed and new.
Like Khadijah, my spirit's unbound,
A healing balm soothing broken hearts all around.

Rumi's flames burn in my stunning element,
A river of light where hope is relevant.
With Maya's storytelling in my veins,
I speak with those who've worn the silent chains.

With no veil to hide my face,
My presence fills this space.
Through every line, a soft embrace,
I soothe the reader, one poem, one grace.

This is my balm, my healing powers,
A person's voice, yours, mine, and ours.

# LEZEL SIMONS

**Lezel Simons is a self-published author of three poetry and prose collections: She Was a Warrior All Along, it all comes back to.., and Love Evol. Inspired by love, poetry has been a companion through trauma, loss, grief, and pain.**

**A widow and mother to two boys, Lezel is also a physiotherapist, writer, and love warrior. Through her words, she seeks to help others heal, grow, evolve, and experience magic.**

# IF POETRY WERE A PERSON
# BY LEZEL SIMONS

If Poetry were a person
they'd smell of vanilla, cinnamon,
ylang ylang and roses
Leave wisps of them in every room
linger in your thoughts
A complex mix of sweet nothings
and stirring truths

They'd pop up uninvited
and know when they should
because life needs them
even when we don't know we do

If poetry were a person
their voice would sing when they speak
Gentle, fluid and deep
Without hearing
you would feel the sound
The type of person who knows strength
because they have been weak
You can't help but miss them
when they're not around

They hide their magic
behind eyes and words
Hoping, no knowing
the right ones will find them there

If Poetry were a person they'd be
an acquired taste
Not easily understood
but exists to understand
The person everyone seeks
when pain finds them

Poetry cries easily
Lives to make others smile and laugh
They see all of you
Recognises what we hide

If Poetry were a person
They'd be poetic without words too
You'll see in them only
what you can see

The type of person you want to know
intimately
If you have ever longed for connection
and intimacy

They'll love you more
than you have ever been loved
and still let you be...
free

If Poetry were a person
Poetry would be
you/me
you and me?

# VINOO NYDOO

Vinoo Nydoo is a retired teacher who has worked with mainstream pupils, adults, and children with special educational needs in cities as diverse as Durban, Cape Town, Port Elizabeth, Bangkok, and London. He is also a freelancer who has had work published in the BBC's Focus on Africa magazine (London) and the Unesco Courier (Paris). He has also contributed substantially to the online content of Colors magazine (Catena Villorba, Italy).

Locally, he has had work published in both You and Drum magazines. Vinoo has also exhibited his graphic art and photographs in Durban, London, and Paris. His most recent exhibition was Intersections and Subsets: An Assignment on Gender and Stereotypes, which ran as part of the Durban International Book Fair - Suncoast, 9-14 August 2023. In addition, Vinoo is also a contributing photographer for Shutterstock, a stock-picture agency.

# POETRY IS NOT DEAD
# BY VINOO NYDOO

It's a mesmerisingly meaningful,
Morning meme
I positioned inside my head.
It's the dark-as-death
Front-page news
I wish I hadn't read.

It's the wondrous way
We work with words.
Giving them the freedom of uncaged birds.
It's the approvals in green
And the warnings in red
And the brilliant colours inside my head.

It's the sidewalk there; that's someone's bed.
It's a wall with a message
Scribbled in red.
And it's that unforgettable poem
My mother read
Before she tucked me into bed.

# CAGED
## BY VINOO NYDOO

The negativity that surrounds us.
The collective attempts to fool us.
The lies they tell us.
The stories they sell us.
The propaganda they feed us
As they tell us they need us...
In spite of all of that,
The worst kind of prison,
Is still the one
We set up for ourselves.

# ZOË-LIN AKKIAH

**Zoë-Lin Akkiah is a 22-year-old BA Honours student at UKZN. Her art and the ability to tell her story and express herself through various mediums have been incredibly liberating in a rapidly changing world and highly integrated society. She hopes that her work helps others find a sense of solace, fosters appreciation for the art form, and encourages a deeper internal conversation.**

# A FREER STATE
## BY ZOË-LIN AKKIAH

Midnight blue plateaus and arid lands,
cows and horses and storms of sand.
My eyes perceive what could possibly be
the most miserable place on Earth, or a reflection of me.

The sun sets in its oranges, pinks, and gold;
on my left, a full moon, all bright and bold.
The sky sprinkled with stars, what a picturesque display,
to imagine what the hunters of old might have seen in their
day.

A town content in sugar-coated segregation,
their flag raised in proud condemnation.
Families reside in delusion in their utopia,
a cold village drowning in an unsustainable euphoria.

The wisdom I have harvested from desolate lands
resides in me and forever stands.
I find solace in my silence, in the desert of my mind,
where rain may find me from time to time.

It was on the road I found myself,
an understanding hidden amongst the shrubs and acres of
mesa.
Here is where my secrets lie, and my problems decrease in
size.
Here is where a part of my soul took flight,
to find rest with !Xu, a sweeter voice I hear,
a guide that never tires, a love that always perseveres.

# THE SWEETEST CONTRADICTION
## BY ZOË-LIN AKKIAH

You are the silver lining
and the thunderstorm,
the darkness of the night
and the morning dawn,
a fine-tuned guitar
in a heavy metal song,
the poison and the cure,
the right and the wrong,
the sweetest contradiction,
the one that tops them all.
Is that even when I hate you,
all I mean is I love you more.

# VANESSA GOVENDER

Vanessa Govender is an Occupational Therapist with a deep passion for helping individuals overcome their challenges. She works in education, supporting children with special needs.

In addition to her career, Vanessa is a devoted music enthusiast who sings, and an avid writer of poetry and short stories. She believes in the therapeutic power of these arts and regularly incorporates them into her practice to enhance the well-being of the children she treats. Vanessa has a positive outlook on life, despite having lived through many dark days. Her challenges have made her stronger and led her to put down her life experiences in words. She has one published short story and three poems, with the dream of publishing a compilation of her poetry and children's storybooks.

Her love for music is profound, and she hopes to convert one of her poems into a song. Vanessa truly believes in the words of Beethoven, "Music can change the world."

# MUSIC MAKES MY HEART SING
# SONNET BY VANESSA GOVENDER

Music makes my heart sing and dance all around
Rhythm pulsing through my mind and body
Twisting and thumping all over the ground
Feeling the beat, I join with somebody

I know too well this beautiful jingle
Helping me remember the day I met with my love
A tune to which my body would tingle
The angels join this frenzy from above

A new song brings with it another mood
That time I felt like I was losing you
A melody to which I sat and brood
Only to find you were always so true

You, singing my praises from mountains high
My heart skips a beat, and I want to fly

# THE BEACH
# BY VANESSA GOVENDER

Tide after tide
You ebb and flow
Time after time
It goes so slow

The warmth of the sun
And the sand on my feet
Time for some fun
And people to meet

Now you come gushing
For us to meet
Roaring and crushing
At my feet

At the end of the days
I sit and watch
As you merge with the rays
A sight nothing can match

# ANTHEE RAMLUCKEN SUKAI

**Anthee Ramlucken Sukai is a visual artist who also loves writing poetry when inspired. Weaving a story into a poem or a painting, is what inspires her. Growing up in those dark apartheid days left an impact of secrecy where one always had to be careful about their thoughts, words, and deeds. However, artistic expression has always been a natural outlet for her emotions.**

**Anthee is a South African female of Indian descent, with her own trials and triumphs. In her early years, she trained and worked as a Textile Designer, then continued to study through UNISA, until she achieved her Fine Arts Degree. Much later in life, to her great joy, she was given an opportunity to volunteer at the Durban Art Gallery and eventually became a Museum Officer at the Ethekwini Local History Museum. Coming from a quiet, secluded life in her early years, Anthee retains the ability to enjoy solitude and contemplation. Books were her companions. In her twenties, music, friends, and a bohemian Rock and Roll lifestyle broadened her perspective, leading her to break free from conformity.**

**Her journey of self-discovery led her to a spiritual master, strengthening her belief that we are spiritual beings having a human experience. Now, in this phase of her life, Anthee continues to embrace the wonder around her, she continues to grow and learn, realising that in the present, only gratitude matters. .**

# BALLAD OF THE BRIDE
## ANTHEE RAMLUCKEN SUKAI

It was a hundred years ago
She waited in her bridal gown;
Princess of a nomadic tribe
Regal dress with jewel and crown

"What happened here?" The family quizzed
The psychic closed her eyes in trance
"Weeping wind blows through our house"
"Ahh", the psychic said, taking a chance

"He never came, the groom to be.
She waited in her bridal gown
She sobs now, lonely in this place.
It's her sad sound that makes you frown"

In a prayer, she bade her leave
"Your love awaits beyond the veil
Lost his life on his way to wed"
Weeping wind stilled- love did not fail

# THE WEDDING
# BY ANTHEE RAMLUCKEN SUKAI

We took our vows in the temple of the Gods,
Tremulous and enchanted, more than a little awed,
The gravity of our commitment, solemn and sincere,
Yet, oddly, decreed in some other age or year.
Deities garlanded and cast in stone,
Stood in alcoves so small,
Mysterious and powerful, spiritually so tall,
Blessing us as, side by side, we had our fill
Of a truth within that surely must be His will.
All pride and ego vanquished in the face of gratitude,
Of finding love in a world so destitute,
So afraid of causing pain and suffering,
Asking for mercy and protection as an offering.
Part we had to, but I felt no less a bride,
Bound to you now and forever, I joyously cried.
Later, driving through the dark and moonless night,
The magic remained, never once taking flight.
I sat alone in the pew, yet I had you in my heart,
Never knowing you came searching, never wanting to part.
Wanting to hold in your arms the love that was yours,
On a night when the world sang out
Through windows and doors,
In praise, in joy, in yearning, "Om Nama Shivaya."
And the Lord, in His mercy, granted us our wish.
In another year, on a night like this,
And we vowed yet again on this blissful night
To love and to cherish and to hold hope tight.

# PADMINI GOVENDER

Padmini Govender is a poet with a background in financial accounting, but words have always been her true calling. This year, she became an author. Her debut collection, The Moon Child, features emotional and thought-provoking poetry and prose.

Padmini is also an avid photographer with a keen eye for unique perspectives on the mundane and an absolute lover of nature. Her photographs draw the viewer into her world through beautiful imagery, grounding her in the natural world, which is reflected in both her photography and her writing. Some of her photographs are featured in her book, The Moon Child.

"The following poem, Our Queen, is a tribute to my mum, Kogie. A woman of immeasurable resilience, with a heart of gold - My Queen."

# OUR QUEEN
# BY PADMINI GOVENDER

Snowy white hair gently framing the face,
Now etched with soft wrinkles and a smile.
Her sorrows buried in the depths of her soul,
Hidden from prying eyes; hidden from herself.

Still playfully young at heart,
Strong enough to hold the family
Through the storms of life,
Often rudderless in a leaky boat.

What were her dreams?
Did she want more of life?
We never asked the questions;
It was just how society was.

A woman in a patriarchal world,
Being a wife and mother,
Everything for everyone,
Nothing for herself,

Enduring immense loss
When her life partner fell ill
And later to eternal rest,
As wife and mother and
Everything in between.

She rose, like a Phoenix out of the ash,
In her rise to be the Queen that she is.
She dragged the helpless with her
On the road to restorative healing.

A strong lineage follows her,
Guided with the same love
That once graced her life.
Ancestral matriarchy strong.

No withering wallflowers there,
Brave women in a hostile world,
Women who, in the face of all adversities,
Pulled their families into power.

# PAREIDOLIA
# BY PADMINI GOVENDER

The sky, mesmerizing blue vastness,
With wispy clouds that trail gently,
Or dark and angry with menace of a storm.

This ancient pastime
Brings a stillness to my heart,
Seeing the clouds resemble the random.

There's a word for this, that I still love to do:
Pareidolia – a scientific name for a pleasant pastime.

The beauty is still hypnotic,
A star-filled sky and no moon,
Dawn as it breaks through
In a spectacular sunrise.

A disruptive storm causes chaos,
A hauntingly beautiful sunset.
Cloud-gazing lures me,
To stop for a while,
To rest and ground my soul,
To simply be, in that moment of time.

# SONIA NAIDOO

Sonia Naidoo is a multi-talented poet, author, ghostwriter, photographer, and artist, born and raised in Durban, South Africa. She is engaged to Jaidan Jairaj, a South African actor, model, and businessman.

Her passion for literature blossomed at the tender age of four, nurtured by her mother, Yasmeen Naidoo, who taught her to read and write. Sonia's writing journey began at the age of fifteen, when she and her best friend, Lavasha Naidoo, started crafting short fanfiction stories inspired by their favourite books and movies. During this period, Sonia also turned to poetry as a means of coping with anxiety and depression.

Sonia holds a Higher Certificate in Photography, a Certificate in Business Administration, and Diplomas in Biblical Studies and English Language and Literature. She also runs a freelance photography business called S K Y-Photography.

# EARTH, OUR MOTHER, OUR CHILD
## BY SONIA NAIDOO

Rustling leaves dance on the golden ground.
Specks of nature's offspring's
Catch in the spider webs of my hair.
Ears hear the harmony of her wind.

Grass blades don't cut my fingertips.
God made her the Mother who is soft.
Opening her body to us,
We conquer and spoil.

Her lungs breathe in humanities poison
Gold mines grow upon her rotting limbs.
Impregnated with the sins of man,
Her womb fills with polluted water.

Flowers bloom within her draught
And concrete towers cannot overcome.
She dances in the moonlight's gaze,
She is the Mother,
We were born to raise.

# SEVANI SINGARAM

Dr. Sevani Singaram is a health professional, PhD graduate and an MBA graduate. She is the author of The disappearance of Amy Nel-a South African mystery and Short stories and poetry by a South African, both of which are available from Amazon.com. Her email address is drsevanisingaram@gmail.com

# ABOUT TIME
# BY SEVANI SINGARAM

The rat race presses on everyday,
drawing millions of people into a never ending game.
But, beware!
You can be easily ensnared into a nightmare.
Everyone is rushing. Everyone is planning.
Everyone is chasing. Everyone is frantic.
Society makes us believe that the more we do with our time,
the bigger will be our dime.
So, we neglect our well-being to get bigger and better things.
But, amidst the chaos, we must realise that time is not ours to
conquer, and before we were created,
our days were numbered.
Time may have a different meaning for every human being.
To the one dying, they want more of it.
To the one despondent, they want less of it.
To the one cherishing a little while,
they probably wish it could stand still.
Everyone has their own timeline, according to God's plan.
Can you not fathom,
that even the ocean moves to it's own rhythm?
People may take eons to accomplish a goal while others take
half the time to have something to show .
You see, in the end it will never be about how much you
crammed into your time.
You need to realise that, it's about time!

# FARAH MESSI

Farah Messi, 26, is an author, poet, feminist, and fiancée. She is the published author of thexchild, an anthology of poems about heartbreak and healing. An avid reader, cat mom, and woman in STEM, Farah was born in Durban, raised in Joburg, and found her rhythm in Cape Town. She has so much love to share.

# MONEY IS POWER
# BY FARAH MESSI

If kindness could be turned into gold,
I would be in a penthouse suite.
I'd be sleeping on silk sheets, satin slippers on my feet,
sitting at tables where they've reserved my seat.
If kindness could be turned into gold,
I'd wake up in a glass house watching the sunrise
with my best friend next to me, getting lost in his eyes;
knowing I wouldn't want it otherwise.

If kindness could be turned into gold,
I'd see to it that my mother never grows old.
I would buy back the house that we sold.
Our home would never again be cold.
I'd have friends and we'd sit on the balcony
and laugh about the jokes we told,
the tricks we played, the mistakes we made.
We'd talk about the times we prayed
for all the things we have,
for the life we find laid out in front of us.

If kindness could be turned into gold.
But it can't. And even if it could, it wouldn't.
Because life is cruel.
Life has rules. Rules that aren't taught in schools.
They aren't taught in churches, in camps,
in overnight conferences.
They're unclear rules
that are whispered to you in confidence.
In offices, between colleagues.
On bathroom floors, between friends.
In bed, between lovers.

If kindness could be turned into gold...
But it cannot. That's one of the rules.
And so every kind person is forced to be cruel too.
Kindness compels us to put down our tools, call it a day.
Kindness could never make that person stay.
Too much kindness pushes people away.
If kindness were gold, it'd lead people astray.
Our moral compasses would be in disarray.

But be that as it may
if kindness could be turned into gold,
maybe then I'd finally have a hand to hold.

# VEE DILRAJH

Vee Dilrajh is a **64-year-old** male from Durban, KwaZulu-Natal. By profession, he is a Food Scientist at the Durban University of Technology. While science fascinates him, he finds his true balance in the field of arts, which has been his lifelong passion. Over the years, he has made significant contributions to various artistic pursuits.

Vee has been writing poetry since the age of 15, building a solid collection that spans five decades of work. Some of his poems have been read on national radio, although he has yet to have any published works. In addition to poetry, he has written numerous original songs, although none have been commercially released to date.

A talented musician, Vee is an active performer in his own band, where he plays multiple roles, including guitarist, singer, drummer, and keyboard player. He is also an experienced audio and lighting engineer, running his own small company that provides audio and lighting services for live events.

Vee's writing is deeply inspired by nature, relationships, politics, love, and tragedy. He writes from the core of his emotions, especially when truly inspired, and hopes that those who experience his work find enjoyment and resonance in it.

# PLASTIC BAND
# BY VEE DILRAJH

Look around you. Plastic everywhere!
What are you wearing?
Some fancy plastic-rubber footwear?
What do you sit on?
A white plastic chair?
Here, sip on some water.
From your plastic bottle container?
We are plastic consumers,
Never-ending, nobody cares!

Don't go singing in the rain.
There's plastic in the air.
It's raining plastic everywhere.

As it becomes clearer,
But for how much longer?
Living in a world covered in plastic.
The bag's over your head, slowly suffocating.
Until Earth becomes a ball of bubble wrap,
Tied up with a plastic band.
Banned too late?

# STILL YOUR CHILD
# BY VEE DILRAJH

Ma,
Before you died, I spoke to you.
I said it's alright for you to go.
But I lied, our hard and last goodbye.
I never forgot that, as I cried.
I'm still your child.

I remember the day
You held the fragile hand of a young boy,
Trying to cross a busy street –
I was fearful, standing safely by your side.
Today, as I search for your fragile hand,
Help me cross life's lonely streets.
I am fearful, but you are alongside.
I'm still your child.

The times I cried when I was hurt,
Waiting for you to kiss away my tears, my comfort.
Hugs and love in an endless stream,
Encouraging me on to build new dreams,
Never judging or giving up on me.
Always there, a part of my journey.
I'm still your child.

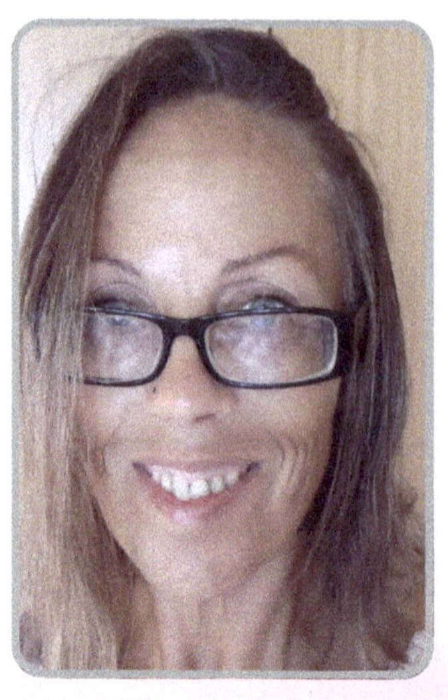

# DONNA-MARIE

Donna-Marie is a passionate poet who has been writing for many years. She has been published several times in the past, but this time she has truly grown as a writer by exploring genres she is not accustomed to. Despite the challenges, she is having the time of her life and hopes that the pieces she has written resonate deeply with readers, as they are written with them in mind.

Currently, Donna-Marie is working on a novel, with hopes that this one will be published. She has written many books in the past, but never dared to try and publish them. Unfortunately, these works are now lost, scattered by the wind after several moves. Nonetheless, she remains hopeful that one day, with God's blessing, she will be able to share her world with readers in the future.

# AFRICAN NARRATIVE
# BY DONNA-MARIE

A vista! In front of me,
the image of fields gently rolling,
The baobab grows strong!
I hear the twang of the isitolotlo blowing.
Brown grasses and thorn trees lying in the wide veld of Africa,
Sound waves above the cicadas,
from Cape Town to Madrasa.

Here we see the leopard sprint, slamming in buck hoof,
showing the stampede of buffalo where the elephant stands,
traditionally invoking hazel soils to become hazy,
my skin sizzles with sweat, my body in taffeta.
The shining sun with a red-eyed dove,
while the wise woman is my anima.

In this wild, I am bowled away as the ibis screams,
cajoling the blood lily to grow,
she, a splash of earthy reds, after a hunt.
Going into fields littered with white daisies,
swaying soundlessly in nature,
As the carrion picks the countryside clean,
like a dream, but a massacre.

All wildlife bound in time, countless times,
in synch, in physical rhyme, bowing to the wild dogs,
that the lion watches, full of a meal, giving some,
allowing the will of the wild, and me, an African child,
my mind like a digital camera.
Watching wild seas who release the decrees of seagulls,
their voices a-clamour.

The vast myriad of stars that glitter in morning's silver mists,
as fire is sowing the seeds of African woodburn.
While seas align on sleepy shores, foaming.
In jungles and bush, a delegation of so many clans,
hard and strong, that belong in view.
South to north of Africa, our dreams surrendered,
and under a Mopani tree, they renewed!

# SANJANA SINGH

Sanjana Singh is a twenty-two-year-old aspiring author in South Africa. Sanjana is passionate about writing, well-versed in creative arts, with a knack for writing from various perspectives. Sanjana's work has been featured in several notable publications.

# THE MOON
## BY SANJANA SINGH

A human resembles a moon.
Just like the moon has to go through phases,
So do we.
Each phase is a new chapter, born from the previous.
Every moon can only shine in darkness,
And so this is our reflection.
When darkness surrounds us, it is in our nature to shine.
Even in the darkest of times, our beauty is witnessed
By the lost wanderer, the glistening lake,
The howling wolf, and even the woke owl.
In every human resides a moon
To guide those around them.
We just need to remember
That we are not the end of the beginning,
But the beginning of the end.
We are beautiful.

# YASEEN ADAM

Yaseen Adam is a filmmaker by profession, with a background in scriptwriting and poetry. Hailing from Durban, South Africa, he remains deeply connected to his roots despite his travels abroad. Yaseen exclusively writes poetry centered on Love, driven by his natural passion for the subject. His work aims to inspire hope in others, encouraging them to never give up on Love. He is grateful for the opportunity to share his creative journey.

# LOVE DON'T LEAVE ME
## BY YASEEN ADAM

Visions of love are innumerable,
Yet true love within hearts is measurable.
Animosity resides deeply in some
for those who have found it,
For how does the hater find love,
swarming in dejection?
Leaving their ego aside and drowning
in the ocean of pure, blissful love...
For love gives life to death...
...for death gives life to love.

# TAMIA MOONSAMY

Tamia Moonsamy has always considered words her greatest passion and defence. She began writing poetry in high school when she realised it was the perfect outlet for expressing her suppressed emotions. Poetry became a way for her to release her thoughts without judgement, no matter how intrusive they could sometimes be. In today's world, it can be difficult to voice opinions or express oneself without fear of backlash from society. However, poetry offers the opportunity to say what's on one's mind in a completely safe environment. Tamia believes that poetry is a powerful medium to reach people who are struggling with their emotions but have no outlet. As such, her favourite saying is, "I write for you." Though her poetry stems from her own experiences, others who are emotionally struggling can relate to her words. Strong and simple emotion-triggering words evoke a sense of shared experience between Tamia and her readers. And that, she believes, is her greatest superpower – simplicity.

# PROCESS
## BY TAMIA MOONSAMY

Draft after draft, I write with no remorse.
The more I pen, the longer the course.
No destination, just a journey I'm on.
Will I reach the end? The question is born.

Edit after edit, still no sign of closing.
The mind racing, while the body's dosing.
No destination, just a journey I longed for.
Will I reach the end? The question is heartsore.

Version after version, you'd think it's done.
The mocks and goads, are all but fun.
No destination, just a journey I dread.
Will I reach the end? The question is dead.

The final run, nothing left to send.
Is my story ready? Will they like the end?

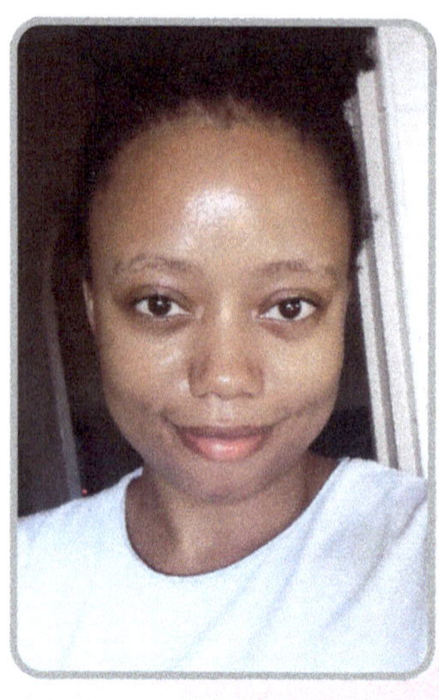

# STHUTHUKILE MKHIZE

**Sthuthukile Mkhize is a talented writer, artist, editor, blogger, and poet. Her passion for writing began in high school, where she spent every afternoon reading at her local library. Her poems have been featured in multiple publications, including The Paper Trail Literary Journal and the 2025 anthology South African Verses.**

**Sthuthukile currently works as a freelance editor, helping authors and poets reach their full potential. When she is not editing manuscripts or essays, she spends her time writing in her journal or on her personal blog. She also volunteers as a Trauma Debriefer at her local police station, ensuring that trauma victims are treated with care and consideration. She plans to publish a poetry collection in the future.**

# BUS TO NEW ORLEANS
## BY STHUTHUKILE MKHIZE

In the third row on a bus to New Orleans,
I looked about, and seeing no one around,
I left my dream, there on the window seat,
In an old shoebox I'd packed carefully.
It took me a while, but eventually, I fit everything:
A rhinestone tiara and crumpled letters
Addressed to a love I can never have,
Some seashells I collected from the beach,
Every book I've ever read,
Every line of poetry that I wrote in the throes of agony,
A single pearl strung on gold string,
A dress the most brilliant shade of blue you've ever seen.
I didn't cry as I stepped out in the city,
My heart light and no longer heavy...
For once, oh, for once I was free.

And that's when I saw you.

Heart tender like a newborn shoot,
In your hands, an old shoebox
That I knew was carefully packed, beautifully painted,
Clutched to your chest.
In your eyes, a softness untainted yet,
Suddenly, all too clearly, I knew what to do.
I turned on my heels and sped
through the streets,
And chased after my dream
That I left behind on the third row,
On the window seat,
On a bus to New Orleans.

# KINJAL VITHAL

**Kinjal Vithal is a woman who has been both harmed and healed by words. She places great value on thoughtful exchanges, preferring to get to the heart of matters rather than skimming over things. Writing has brought her closer to her creative community. Her imagery is inspired by time spent in nature, as well as her love for people and animals.**

# TREE OF LIFE
# BY KINJAL VITHAL

Tree of Life
Magnificent, powerful and alive.
Creating universal links and connecting each of us.
Every leaf a person, reflecting love back and forth.
Each branch an extension of a different place.
Intentions behind even a single action may seem insignificant,
but it adds and subtracts from this network we call life.
Exceedingly blessed are we who love deeply,
nourishing our relationships down to the roots.
When I listened, the tree said:
Spend time in nature,
we can feel more deeply and speak freely there.
Let the breeze sweep you, I will hold on tight.
Sway and trust that you are safe.
Let the rains cleanse you, and let the sun help you grow.
Appreciate my offerings: flowers, fruits, and oxygen -
they will help sustain you.
Try to create more than you consume.
Live actively instead of accepting life as it is, the storms end.
Do take care of me, as the weather around us is changing.
Some of you destroy precious leaves also sadly even stems
and whole branches, you are only hurting yourself.
Live in harmony, working together.
Your ever-present, eternally loving and all-feeling
Tree of Life.

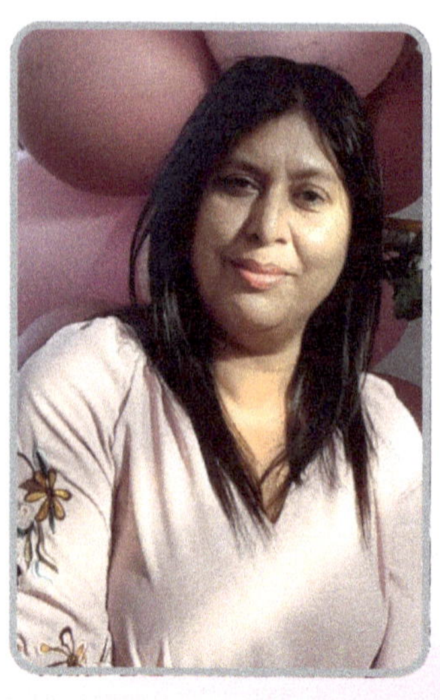

# ZAHIDA WAHAB

**Zahida Wahab is an educator, published author, and poet, as well as a community and social activist. She serves as the public liaison officer for the Chatsworth Regional Hospice Association and is a former trustee of the same organisation. Zahida has also worked as a columnist and radio presenter. Additionally, she is an author and Funda Leader with Nal'ibali, the National Literacy Campaign.**

# COLOURS OF CHANGE
## BY ZAHIDA WAHAB

When storm clouds gather, as they often do,
Painting the sky a dismal grey from azure blue,
I turn to thoughts of the changing seasons:

Winter, with its icy chill, magnificent and beautiful still.
Spring, with flowers of multi-coloured hues,
Trees so green, and skies so blue.
Summer, with its warmth and sunny days,
Bringing cheer, and lazy ways.
But Autumn is perhaps the greatest lesson,
Revealing to me that despite the change,
beauty still prevails.
Just as the golden leaves falling from the trees,
There is hope to set me free,
To await the spring, when I will once again bloom,
Casting off the shadows of despair and gloom.

I will embrace the changes, for they set me free,
Shaping me into the person I was meant to be.
I sit in reverence in God's glory,
For He is the greatest author of my story.
He is the greatest artist, painting the sky
With fiery, resplendent colours
of a glorious sunset and sunrise.
One a beginning, and the other an end,
But both replete with beauty that knows no end.

# WHEN STORM CLOUDS GATHER<br>BY ZAHIDA WAHAB

When storm clouds gather and your world turns dark,
Look deep within you for that eternal spark.
Whisper words of hope and let the glow shine bright,
Pick up your sword and get ready to fight.

This battle that rages is not yours alone,
You fight for those whose voices are not their own.
You fight so that a child knows their future is bright,
Your fight is for all that is true and right.

You fight so that a woman can escape
the shackles of abuse, and blinding rage,
so she doesn't end up as a mere statistic
on a newspaper page.

You fight so that those oppressed are given hope,
Can hold their heads high,
Emboldened with the strength to cope.

So never give up, warrior friend,
For your valour will be the light that never ends.
It will guide others through their darkest night,
And inspire them to join the fight.

And when the battle's finally won,
And the storm clouds have parted, one by one,
You'll stand victorious, with a heart full of pride.
So never give up, no matter how tough the fight.
The darkest night will eventually turn into a day so bright,
And in your light, others will find their strength
to rewrite their story and begin once again.

# VISHNU KRISTNA

**Vishnu Kristna is a published author specialising in poetry. He holds a Bachelor of Commerce degree in Marketing from the University of South Africa and also runs his own small business, PRINT TECH DESIGNS.**

**Stepping Stones is his first published anthology of poetry, where he reflects on the struggles he faced while growing up and navigating life. It explores how he overcame these challenges and persevered through adversity to publish his first book, a proud accomplishment for him.**

**He has also contributed to an anthology of poems and short stories entitled South African Verses. Vishnu plans to write more poetry books and is keen to explore other genres, such as fiction novels and an autobiography that will highlight the unique aspects of his life's journey. In addition to his writing, Vishnu has ventured into the world of acting. In his spare time, Vishnu enjoys staying fit by going to the gym. He also enjoys reading biographies and listening to podcasts that offer insights into the minds of famous and successful people.**

**You can find his book online at www.amazon.com and bookle.co.za. For more information or any questions relating to purchasing the book directly or providing feedback, Vishnu encourages positive reviews and can be contacted via email at poeticxpress001@gmail.com.**

# POETIC REVOLUTION
## BY VISHNU KRISTNA

Over the centuries one thing remains in common,
People for centuries have been etching their life experiences
onto the canvas of a page

Nobody expresses their raw, unedited emotions
better than a poet in touch with every fibre of their being
If you cut a poet
You don't just into his skin or flesh
But you cut into their very deep heart

And he turns that knife into a pen and uses his blood as ink
Retaliating in his mind that spills onto the page with words
that can penetrate and hurt the very essence of your being

A poet finds solace in the lines between a page
Between those lines they are available to express
their true nature freely without remorse or regret

One thing about POETS
is that they can never hide their true feelings
Whether it be directed at them or in the world at large
They always give their uncensored views
no matter if it fits the mainstream narrative or not

POETS bleed on the page for others
to read and understand their pain

POETS leave an everlasting impression on your mind
when you realize the depths of your love
is just scratching the surface of love with them

POETS tell you that you are never more lonely than them
No matter how alone you can be at that time

POETS always wear their hearts on their sleeves
So they can never even try to hide their true emotions

POETS see the world through different lenses than other
people
They somehow can see through the bullshit
and view the truth of the situation for what it truly is

POETS write love poems from the heart
That can take you on a magical journey all over the world
and bring you back feeling ecstatic
right to the pages in your book

How do I know all this
Because I am of course a Poet!
As long as there are people on earth
And there are feelings to be felt
There will be words written on life and strife
From the poetic wordsmiths from around the world

Poetry always breathes new life
Creating new colours
To brighten this life's dull existence
Into a beautiful, colourful and memorable experience

So POETS unite!
The world needs you
Now more than ever.

# RICHARD J. MANN

**Richard J Mann is a writer specialising in political satire and humour, known for blending sharp wit with insightful commentary. He began his literary journey by writing short stories, unexpectedly winning first prize in a South African Writers' Circle short story competition many years ago, an achievement that marked the beginning of his creative career.**

**Richard's blog, The Scuffle Continues, has earned significant recognition, ranking among the top 50 satirical blogs on the internet. He has also written for major publications, including Daily Maverick, The Citizen, The Sowetan, and Staffrider, and contributed a story to an SABC radio programme. Despite the challenges faced by freelancers in the industry, his work continues to make an impact. In addition to his online presence, Richard has published five satirical books on Amazon Kindle and has ventured into TikTok and YouTube, where he offers his unique perspective on current affairs.**

**Currently, Richard is working on his sixth satirical book and co-authoring a collection of short stories titled People of the Valley (working title).**

# FIRST SIGHT
## BY RICHARD J. MANN

Nothing so boring
as a queue,
The minutes stretched and would not break.
Then I saw you.
A face I've dreamt and can't remember where,
Your eyes knew mine from time I can't recall,
I joked, you smiled,
The lights purred softly and
the room took wing,
And every other face was pale or grey,
The minutes coalesced, stood still,
Caught in surprise.
Whatever time may take or add,
You are forever framed in light.

# REMEMBERING
## BY RICHARD J. MANN

Remembering
Warm earth steaming after rain,
That blue, first morning.
And the soil new born.
The sun,
Egg yellow as the farm's new laids,
Bird-blossomed trees,
Geese like a farewell over them,
A lullaby of waters,
Coloured in the clouds and sky,
A flash of silver, darting swift.
These things and all they sing
The ache of memory on the wing

# BIANCA NIKITA

**Bianca Nikita is an avid reader whose enthusiasm for literature has sparked an interest in writing. In addition to her everyday job in pharmaceutical manufacturing, she serves as a literary influencer and reviewer for various publishing companies. Bianca is the creator of a Social Media Management company designed to help authors, publishers, and other book enthusiasts expand their presence. Her expertise encompasses content creation, social media management, administration, and marketing.**

**Since childhood, she was enchanted by the adventures that books offer, and this love for reading and writing has continued into her adult years. Lately, Bianca has started to explore and convey her experiences in the literary realm, perpetually motivating others with her passion for literature.**

**IG: bee.with.the.books**

# A WRITER'S CHAOS
# BY BIANCA NIKITA

How do you express your emotion?
You use your words.
So, we bleed our pain onto pages,
Etching our tragedies into every surface.
We sing songs of our love,
and scribble tales of its beauty.
We rhyme our betrayals,
And scratch over the empty promises.

We don't know how to express our emotions,
So, we write.
Our lives become art,
Words carried through generations.

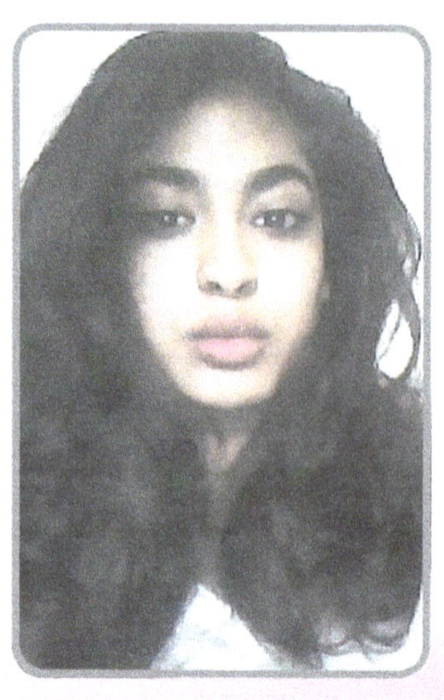

# NIKKI NAICKER

**Nikki Naicker is a young lady who finds joy in spending time in nature and embraces creative ways to express her life. Her hobbies include photography, writing, and gardening, each providing a unique outlet for her artistic and reflective nature.**

# I WRITE
# BY NIKKI NAICKER

I can't sleep when a flood of words and stories
flow through my mind.
I stay up all night but I can't seem to rest my mind.
Then, in the AM, when my thoughts go wild,
I pick up a pen and start to write.
I put down an emotion.
I let my emotions flow through the ink in my pen,
Like the blood flows through my veins,
And the thoughts through my mind.
I write a life for me.
I write a lot.
I write while I eat.
The food fills my body, but the words fill my mind.
I don't mind, it's a one-of-a-kind experience to feel the might
of creativity take charge of my mind.
So, I write.
I write.
I write whatever comes to mind.
When my mind is full and endlessly bound to fight me,
I pick up a pen and write.
Then I put my pen down and let my thoughts go free.
I write.
I write for the sanity of my mind and the serenity of my soul.
I write to feel awake and whole.
I write to put the past to sleep and awaken the future.
I write because, through the craziness of my emotions and
thoughts, comes a beautiful piece of work that inspires others
to feel their emotions.
I write for life.
I write joy.
I write from sadness.
I write what comes to mind.
I write.

# BUSISIWE NGWENYA

**Busisiwe Ngwenya is the author of four short story books, Triumph of a Deserving Person, Waiting For Me, Hitting Fifty in Style, and A Score to Settle, as well as a memoir titled I Am, Me: A PK's Life and a poetry collection called Bound by the Womb, all of which are available on Amazon Kindle.**

**Some of her stories and poems have been published in anthologies and other publications.**

**Busisiwe holds a B Tech in Corporate Administration, a Short Story Writing certificate, and an Executive Development Programme certificate. She has worked for various government agencies and the dtic. She is a member of Gauteng LITASA, the Excellency Growth Club, Tshwane Authors, and the LCSA Health and Wellness Programme.**

# MY BELOVED
## BY BUSISIWE NGWENYA

I was lost and heartbroken,
Heart shattered into glass pieces,
Eyes puffy and swollen,
I was spent and couldn't shed any more tears.

You picked me up,
Swept the pieces together lovingly,
Embraced me tenderly,
Soothed my broken being.

I had never felt so cherished before.
In your eyes, I saw beauty,
It reflected brightly,
A thing I never thought I possessed.

Your strength anchored me,
Your gentle arms enfolded me,
I felt sheltered,
I was seen,
I was worthy of love,
I deserved to be here,
I was needed,
I was cherished.

It was time to let go of the past,
To embrace the future with you.
The hurts and cruelty had no home here,
You exuded peace,
My beloved.

You deemed me worthy where none did.
You are my rock,
My being,
My reason to breathe.

I surrender to you.
Forever we shall be.

# NEERMALA DEVI MOODLEY

Neermala Devi Moodley, born in Merebank and a former resident of Umkomaas for 28 years, now resides in Gauteng. A passionate soul, Neermala has always found solace in expressing herself through the art of poetry, crafting words that resonate deeply with her spirit. For her, poetry is not just an expression but 'Food for the Soul,' a way to connect with her innermost thoughts and feelings.

Her journey has been marked by a soulful search, driven by a relentless passion for self-growth and a desire to inspire through her words. Neermala believes that the highest calibre of a person is defined by respect, self-discipline and character, virtues she holds dear and strives to embody in all aspects of her life.

Her dedication to this path reflects her unwavering commitment to both personal and creative evolution, making her a voice of inspiration for others who seek to find meaning and purpose through the power of words.

# PASSION FOR HUMANITY
## BY NEERMALA DEVI MOODLEY

Born with a purpose, fulfil it!
Identification to a fruitful journey,
Realisation has it: "I'M ALIVE!"
Yes, alive, detecting my own intuition,
Greater than just a thought, awaits its fruits to be born.
Birth to an amazing reality,
As the fruits of its action bear truth in
Unity, equality, compassion, love, and spirituality.
A rainbow embracing love for the human race,
An umbrella sheltering all from the sweltering sun's rays,
And the torrential rain that drenched you,
Into absorption of a breath of freshness, that I'm alive.
Direct this energy to your call to evolve.
See this evolution materialise and manifest
In the human race,
Love for another's growth in this lifetime.
"Purposeful"
Never to be denied, derailed,
or even dead without living it to fruition.
Imagine every morsel served, every drop quenching a thirst,
Every light from within lit brightly, so that darkness dies.
Imagine being selfless to all humanity,
No discrimination,
No racism,
No colour, no creed,
No prejudice.
Only the heart that loves the human race,
Love without conditioning, without hesitation,
without boundaries.
Not that which the eye sees, or the ear hears,
Or is judged by the mind,
But the "Echo of one's soul,"
Yearning, full of love, to fulfil the quest
Of the beauty of every living being to evolve,
To humanity's glory and grace of being alive,
Staying alive, and living alive, not dead,
in "One's living years."

# VIJAYAN VENGADACHELLAM

**Vijayan Vengadachellam is a young male poet who is deeply passionate about writing poetry that reflects emotions and personal experiences. He is dedicated to advocating for those who suffer in silence, using his writing as a means to provide a voice for the voiceless. Writing offers Vijayan an escape from the harsh realities of the world, allowing him to enter a dreamlike state that brings peace to his mind and heart, relieving him from the burdens he carries.**

**One of his proudest achievements is the creation of a deeply meaningful poem titled "And Yet She Was Blamed!", which he considers one of his best works. He hopes that readers will resonate with its message and find a connection to its themes.**

**A quote that guides Vijayan in life is: "Don't let your past mishaps blackmail your present to ruin a beautiful future."**

# MY ANJELLA, ABOVE...
## BY VIJAYAN VENGADACHELLAM

I now reminisce in this silent room,
which was once filled with your laughter,
because it shall always remind me
of what true happiness felt like…
I now reminisce on times you scolded me,
correcting the path I walked on,
to now realise I'm here, longing for you to scold me,
as I am now lost on this path ever since you left,
so, "Ma, scold me! Pleaseee…"

I now reminisce the morning you told me you are leaving,
a voice I barely recognised,
like it was the 'devil's work,' however,
I felt closer to 'God' ever since that morning…
I now reminisce our late-night prayer sessions
to the one above for each other,
without knowing shortly thereafter
I shall kneel alone, praying to You,
My one above…

I now reminisce about tugging my arm under yours,
overdosing on your warmth and comfort,
which drugged me to sleep for hours,
to now overdosing on tablets with the hope of even being
granted a nap, trying to escape the memory of you…

I now catch myself reminiscing every day,
trying to relive every moment I shared with you,
shedding a tear or two, wishing to hold your hand while
going for a walk on a never-ending road…
I'm glad I can have memories of us, which exist in my head,
even though no memories are made anymore,
and I will forever question,
"How did we overcome so many storms together,
yet a raindrop broke us apart?"

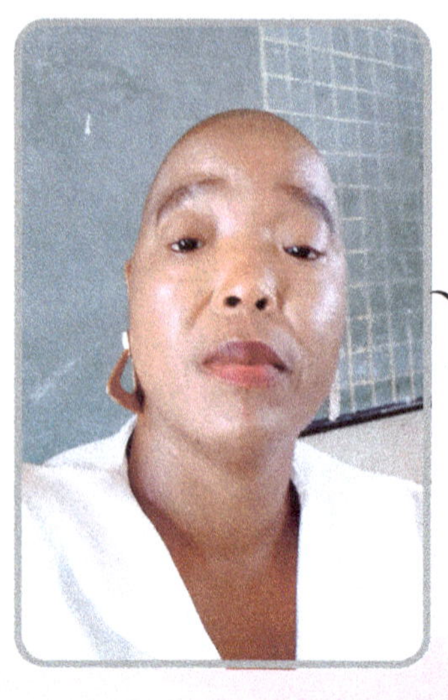

# NOKANYISO MSANI

Nokanyiso Msani was born in March 1979 in a rural area called Amandawe, near Scottburgh. She began her early education at Amandawe Primary School. From a young age, she was eager to help her classmates with their educational challenges, which sparked her passion for becoming an educator.

Coming from a poor family, Nokanyiso was compelled to start working before pursuing tertiary education. She worked in various supermarkets in Umzinto, using the money she earned to fund her studies. Through distance learning at UNISA, she worked hard and completed her Bachelor of Education degree in 2013. She is now a qualified teacher.

# NOT DEAD YET
## BY NOKANYISO MSANI

Not dead yet.
Who says I'm dead?
Who forgets me?
I'm all over like a stray dog,
Echoing like thousands of
mountains.

I intrude hearts like sharp lightning.
Who suffocates me?
I roar like a hungry lion.
Might not be physical or visible,
but can tame the world's imaginations.
Not dead yet.

I'm a giant, a pillar,
I heal the souls,
I revive the souls.
Who can die if I'm still alive?
Who can lose hope
when I'm still fighting?
How can I die in times of need?

How can I disappear?
When our youth turns into murderers,
sinks in drugs,
future leaders perish,
future mothers vanish.
Not dead yet.

Might be limbless, shapeless,
but powerful.
I can shake the world,
shake crowds,
save worlds.
I am not dead yet.

# SAROJ MOODLEY

Saroj Moodley lives in Durban, KwaZulu-Natal. She holds a B.A. degree, an LLB degree, and an LLM degree. Currently, she runs her own consultancy and serves as a Teaching Assistant at UNISA College of Law.

Saroj has a passion for reading, writing poetry, walking, and gardening. She writes struggle poetry, focusing on what she observes and how she feels about those observations. Her first book, The Final Onslaught, was published in November 2019 on Amazon under the pseudonym "Gentry Shae Potts." The book provides readers with an understanding of the political, economic, and social struggles in South Africa.

During the 2020 lockdown, Saroj wrote a book on Gender-Based Violence titled The Lockdown: You Are Not Alone. The purpose of this book is to shed light on the issue of gender-based violence during South Africa's COVID-19 lockdown. It delves into the brutality of murders and rapes of women and children, which shocked the nation. The book examines the psyche of men who engage in such merciless crimes, as well as their misogynistic behaviour. It also explores why women remain in abusive relationships and offers a safety plan and steps for women to take after leaving an abuser. This book is currently in the process of being published.

# A YEAR TO REMEMBER
# BY SAROJ MOODLEY

A year to remember,
"22nd February 1994."
The family took leave that day
to welcome him.
Little did we realise
that a star,
a star was born.

The nursery was abuzz,
abuzz that day.
Suddenly, someone pointed,
pointed to him and exclaimed,
"Aah, he looks like a little golly walk!"
And everyone laughed.
Little did we know
that our little gollywalk
would be a star,
a star someday.

His talent sprouted
at age three,
when with precision, he hit,
hit the ball,
never missing his target,
spinning his grandma's
when they bowled to him,
urging them to pick up the ball
and bowl to him again,
'cause he knew how to work,
work smart.

And when he took out Virat Kohli,
Visakhapatnam stood still,
and we froze,
as the cricket giant was hooked,
hooked in Senuran's web,
dazzling his opponent
in disbelief.
Aim for the moon,
even if you miss,
you'll land,
land among the stars.

And so it came,
came to fruition.
In the SA 20 in 2023,
Pretoria Capitals, Durban,
the man of the match,
an exhilarating moment
that touched our hearts.

Like a spider spinning,
spinning its web,
with class and precision,
he spun the Sri Lankan SA team,
eighteen-wicket haul,
rising to stardom
amongst screaming crowds.

An invigorating moment,
SA 20, Pretoria Capitals, 2024,
with nerves of steel,
calm and composed,
he brought the opposition
to their knees.
An unforgettable moment,
when he hit sixes behind him,
the crowds were silent in disbelief,
the opposition motionless,
and the commentator
exclaimed to the other,
"Did you see that, AK? Class!"
What a proud moment this was.

Humility affirms the inherent
inherent worth of all persons,
and yes, deeply engraved
engraved in his very soul,
Senuran's humility
jerks you to a sense of reality.
Humbleness to the very core,
like a sudden beam of light,
spinning around the sun.
In every walk of life,
illuminating the true sense,
sense of a star.

# SINOBOM VUTHA

Sinobom Vutha is a talented writer and emerging artist based in Durban, originally from the Eastern Cape. Her writing journey began in primary school, where she developed her skills through participation in reading and writing competitions, sparking a lifelong passion for literature.

Primarily known for her poetry, Sinobom has used her craft to engage with social issues and foster meaningful connections. From 2019 to 2021, she expanded her reach to radio, creating thought-provoking pieces on various topics. In her professional role, she crafts captivating content for social media and writes letters on behalf of management, showcasing her creativity and expertise.

Believing in the power of art to drive social commentary, Sinobom's visual artistry also reflects her commitment to these values. As an emerging visual artist, she has showcased her work at the Kwande Festival and the Menzi Mchunu Gallery, where she contributed a powerful written piece for the theme "Our Democracy, Our Freedom, Our Voices."

Sinobom draws inspiration from everyday interactions, human emotions, and the beauty of nature, with her creative work reflecting a deep commitment to personal expression and social consciousness.

# GOLD
## BY SINOBOM VUTHA

With a heart of gold,
Your actions stripped me bare.
Words rolling off your silver tongue
Were everything I didn't know
I needed to hear.
And I could listen all day and night,
Wherever we are.

I want to hear it all.
The hilarious anecdotes about your loved ones,
The somber retelling of past regrets and mistakes,
The lively proclamations of future hopes and dreams.
The silence as we bask in each other's presence.

I want to hear it all.
Make me understand your golden heart.
Tell me what pushes you to wake up in the mornings.

Hopefully, one day I'll see and understand
Why you trust me with your heart of gold.

# SELWYN ANDERSON

**Selwyn Anderson is a father and grandfather, an ex-construction worker, and now a pensioner who has transformed into a first-time writer and poet.**

**He is HIV positive, having discovered his status 17 years ago, when he was diagnosed with AIDS. His journey has been filled with immense challenges. After the initial shock, which led to suicidal thoughts and attempts due to ignorance, Selwyn's family stood by him, with his mother being particularly outstanding. The title of his book, He Is Our Son, comes from his mother's powerful words, which she shouted at his father in front of the nurses at the clinic.**

**His journey has been one of surprises, pain, anguish, excitement, acceptance, and thankfulness to God Almighty. As a reader, his book takes you through an experience that allows you to walk in his shoes, feeling his pain and sharing in his victory. It will encourage you to reflect on your own life, and by the end, you will understand Selwyn's belief, after more than 17 years, that HIV is not a death sentence but a path to positive living.**

**Selwyn's book, He Is Our Son, is available on Amazon, IngramSpark, and Barnes & Noble.**

# POETRY IS NOT DEAD
# BY SELWYN ANDERSON

Poetry is dead, is what some might say,
And this being the sole reason that we are here today.
As poets, we are not here to attend an obituary,
We are here to proclaim that poetry will be with us eternally.

We use poetry to remind us of times that may have passed,
Nostalgic memories of both pain and pleasure
that did not last.
And we use poetry to portray the way that we might feel,
At times escalating to appear so surreal.

We use poetry to describe the way we may feel about Julius
Malema,
And end up by saying, "Haaibo, weh mama mia."
And even go on to use poetry on Donald Trump,
With some even agreeing that he deserves a thumbs-up.

We show concern about corruption and South Africa,
And the political promises that were made,
are we ever going to see them?
We, South Africans, should not focus on the doom
and even the gloom,
When, as poets, we are gifted with the most prized tool.

The pen is lighter and mightier than any sword,
Who could have ever thought that its amazing power
could be so broad?
It morphed to typewriter, computer, laptop, and more,
Captivating and having us engaged throughout the world.

Poetry is not dead and shall never die,
Especially once read, leaving one with a wry smile.
Poetry is not dead and will never die,
Not with the amount of multitalented, unpublished poets that
we have worldwide.

# BRETT "FISH" ANDERSON

Brett "Fish" Anderson is a lover of words and people and is focused on making the world a better place for all who live in it. He is recently married to the Amazing Amanda and owns the world's most famous stuffed dolphin called No_bob [because he doesn't bob!]. You can follow him from a safe distance @brettfisha on Twitter and Instagram or @brettthefish on Tik Tok where he tends to share most of his words to hopefully inspire, challenge, motivate, mobilise and encourage.

# DON'T BELIEVE THE RUMOUR!
# BY BRETT "FISH" ANDERSON

as i reflected on the obituary i had just read
something didn't quite make sense
it was definitely declaring that Poetry had died
but i am pretty sure
i passed Poetry alive and well
as i wandered aimlessly down the main street
yesterday [when all my troubles seemed so far away]

i remember noticing the effects that Poetry had
on my neighbour as she sipped her tea
while reading from her phone
and if i had been sitting next to her
i might have also witnessed the tears
sliding down her face

i watch lovers find each other
and wars threaten to end
pain evolves into possibility
hope reaches the summit
the decisiveness of death is held at bay
worlds are created
and confusions dissipate

but all of this aside
as subjective observations
might yet prove to be fantastical mirages
the reason that convinces me
that this particular author got it
so tragically and emphatically wrong
is that i know beyond the shadow
of a defiant determined deceitful doubt
that Poetry still lives
as i feel it burning deep within me
clamouring to be let out
so that it may seize the heads and hearts of others
and call them to cast of all of their cumbersome inhibitions
and dance uninhibited and unrestrained
along its sneaky little path

# WHAT'S YOUR STORY?
# BY BRETT "FISH" ANDERSON

you know my name
but do you know my story
if you have never taken the time
to sit with me and break bread
as you listen with ears that seek to know
with a heart that longs to hear
and a spirit that has long ago decided
that whatever it takes
is what it must take
to build the bridge between
wherever you have been
and where we now sit
together
chasing after a together
that holds us as equal
and capable
of writing our story
from this moment on?

# Get in touch with us today

alta@sakurabookpublishing.com
ekta@sakurabookpublishing.com

www.ingramcontent.com/pod-product-compliance
Lightning Source LLC
Chambersburg PA
CBHW042033120726

47911CB00026B/724